READING ABOUT

Going to School

By Jim Pipe

Aladdin/Watts

London • Sydney

At school

2

It is the first day of school.
"I've got butterflies in my
tummy," says Alex.

"Don't worry!" says Mum.
"I'll help you get ready."

Getting ready

"Am I late?" asks Alex.

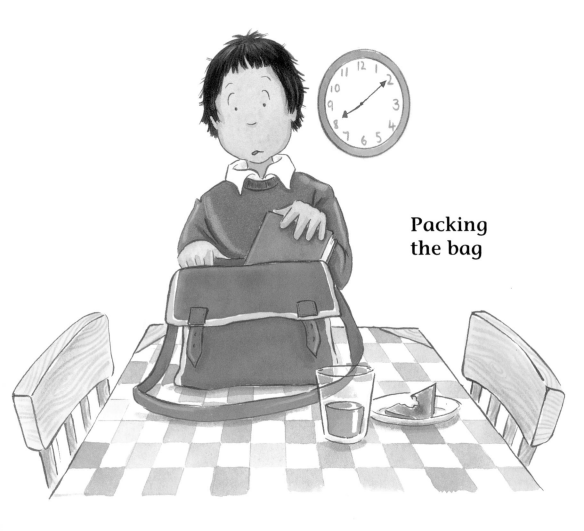

Packing the bag

"Don't worry," says Mum.

"We'll get to school on time."

"Did you pack my pencils and crayons?" asks Alex.

"Don't worry! I packed them in your bag," says Mum. "Let's go!"

Pencil case

Crayons

Pencils

Rubber

Ruler

On the way, Alex sees lots of other children. They wave to each other.

"Will I know anyone?" asks Alex.

"Don't worry!" says Mum.

"Look, there's your friend Sally."

Sally is at the gate with her mum.

School gate

Sally and Alex walk to the classroom with their mums.

"Look at all the things to do," says Alex's mum.

"Yes," says Alex. "This will be fun!"

"See you later," says Mum.

Classroom

The teacher is called Mr Adams.

"Good morning," he says.

"Sit down," says Mr Adams.

"Let's do some writing."

Sitting down

"I forgot my letters," says Sally.

"Don't worry!" whispers Alex.

"We can learn together."

"A is in apple," says Mr Adams,
"and B is in…"

"Banana!" shouts Alex.

"Very good," laughs Mr Adams.

Putting up a hand

Soon it is lunch time.

Alex and Sally see a boy
eating on his own.

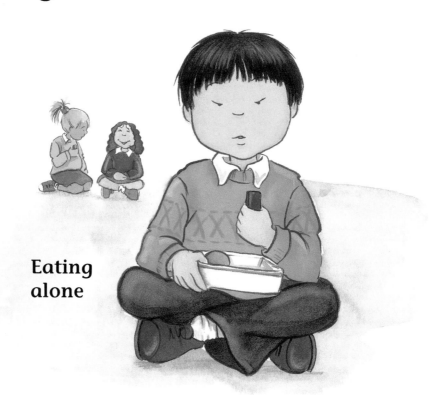

Eating
alone

"Hi," says Alex.
"What's your name?"

"I'm Jin Soo," says the boy.

"Would you like some food from my lunch box?"

Lunch box

"No, thanks, I have my own," says Alex.

"I don't know anyone," says Jin Soo.

"Don't worry!" says Sally.
"Come and play with us."

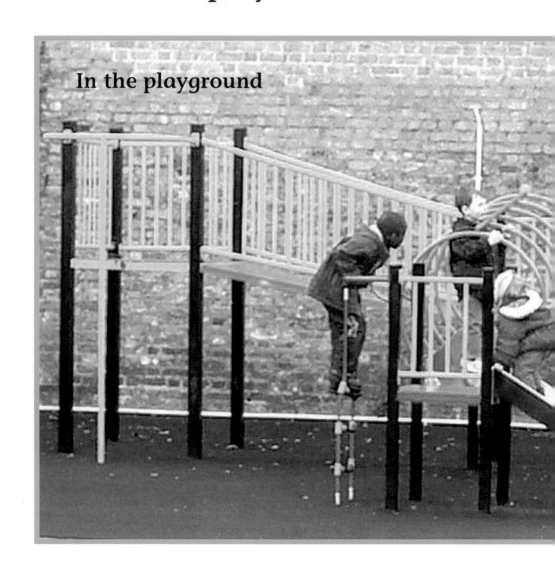

In the playground

So Jin Soo plays with Sally and Alex in the playground.

"This is great fun," says Jin Soo.

After lunch, it is time to paint.
"My brush is too stiff," says Alex.

"Don't worry," says Jin Soo.
"You can use pens
or crayons."

Crayons

So Alex draws a picture
with his pens.

"Very good, Alex," says Mr Adams.

Jin Soo smiles at Alex.

Paints

17

After painting, it is story time.
"I love stories," says Sally.

At the end, everyone gets ready
to go home.

Story time

Dad meets Alex at the gate. "Did you have a good time at school?"

"Yes. I made a new friend, Jin Soo!" Alex waves goodbye to his friends.

Waving goodbye

At home, Mum is waiting.

"Look at my picture," says Alex.

"It's a present for you."

Picture

"Thanks," says Mum. "Where are your butterflies now?" Alex smiles and says, "All gone!"

Here are some words and phrases from the book.

Pack your bag

Put up a hand

Eat lunch

In the classroom

Wave goodbye

Paint a picture

Arrive at school

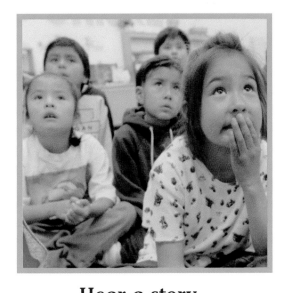

Hear a story

Can you use these words to write your own story?

Did you see these in the book?

Slide

Pencil sharpener

Crisps

Globe

Illustrator: Mary Lonsdale for SGA
Painting page 20: Jamie Eskdale
Picture Credits:
Abbreviations: t – top, m – middle, b – bottom, r – right, l – left, c – centre. 2, 5, 13, 14-15, 16, 17 both, 22, 24tl, 24tr, 24bl – Select Pictures; 8-9, 24br - Catherine Karnow/CORBIS; 10 - Corbis; 18, 23, 24br - Kevin Fleming/CORBIS.